François de Nomé

Mysteries of a Seventeenth-Century Neapolitan Painter

François de Nomé

Mysteries of a Seventeenth-Century Neapolitan Painter

Introduction by

J. Patrice Marandel

Foreword by

Bertrand Davezac

THE MENIL COLLECTION

1991

This exhibtion catalogue was made possible in part by the generous support of elf exploration, inc. and Chase Manhattan Southwest.

Exhibition dates: October 18, 1991 to January 12, 1992

Printed in the United States of America.

Distributed by University of Texas Press
Post Office Box 7819, Austin, Texas, 78713-7819

Library of Congress Cataloging-in-Publication Data

Nomé, François, ca. 1593–ca. 1647.
    François de Nomé : mysteries of a seventeenth-century Neapolitan painter/ introduction by J. Patrice Marandel : foreword by Bertrand Davezac
      p. cm.
    Catalogue of the exhibition organized by the Menil Collection.
    Includes bibliographic references.
    ISBN 0-939594-27-7
    1. Nomé, François, ca. 1593–ca. 1647—Exhibitions. I. Menil Collection, (Houston, Tex.) II. Title.
ND623.N588A4 1991   91-36187
759.5–dc20   CIP

Cover: Detail of François de Nomé's *The Burning of Troy and the Flight of Aeneas* (pl. 8), with permission of the Nationalmuseum, Stockholm.

Contents

Acknowledgments

In the early 1960s, two paintings by François de Nomé, *Interior of a Cathedral* and *A City in Ruins at Night,* entered the collection of Dominique and Jean de Menil. Together with a few other works, they form a small group of European paintings from the sixteenth to the eighteenth century within The Menil Collection. While their selection may have been unsystematic, they are bound together by what the late Charles Sterling noted as a "deeply rooted fascination for them in the collector's personality."

The Museum has recently undertaken a program to isolate single or small groups of works from its collection in exhibitions offering an extended context for that work with the addition of loans from other collections. Such is the intent of this exhibition of François de Nomé, which would not have been possible without the willingness of the following institutions and a private collector to lend important work:

Fitzwilliam Museum, Cambridge
Musée des Arts Décoratifs, Paris
Musée des Beaux-Arts, Montreal
Museum of Fine Arts, Budapest
The Museum of Fine Arts, Houston
Nationalmuseum, Stockholm
North Carolina Museum of Art, Raleigh
The Walters Art Gallery, Baltimore
Yale University Art Gallery, New Haven
Private collection, France.

We are most grateful for their generosity.

J. Patrice Marandel, Curator of European Paintings at the Detroit Institute of Arts, has our deepest appreciation for agreeing to write for this catalogue and then for the outstanding quality of his text. In shifting the perception of eccentricity from applying to the artist but rather to his milieu, which is explored for all its connections to the range of Nomé's subjects and their treatment, he breaks through to the richer consideration of the artist's work as a reflection of the complex and still obscure culture of Naples in the seventeenth century.

Bertrand Davezac curated the exhibition, and we owe to him the perspicacious selection of work that reveals some of the high points of Nomé's achievements as well as the variety of his manners of painting. No small coup is his chancing upon a previously unpublished, but splendid Nomé painting in a private collection in France and arranging its loan to this show. Lauri G. Nelson, Curatorial Assistant, ably and valuably contributed to the realization of this project.

Much is owed to Harris Rosenstein, Editorial Director, who led the editing and planning of this catalogue, and to its designer, Don Quaintance.

Paul Winkler
Director
The Menil Collection

Foreword

"Unduly boosted in our own days, Monsù Desiderio-Nomé was in fact a minor figure, but it was he who opened up a taste in Naples for the weird type of cabinet picture and thus helped to prepare Micco Spadaro's microcosmic views as well as Salvator's Romantic battle-pieces," wrote Rudolph Wittkower in 1958.[1] No small claim for "an unduly boosted minor figure": there was a touch of genius in Salvator Rosa (1615–1673) which catapulted him into the ranks of Italy's leading artists, whose foibles Sir Joshua Reynolds lamented all the more with admiring his sublimity, an artist who in the eighteenth century indeed emblematized the sublime in art.

What can be learned of Nomé's training from the sole documentary evidence that has emerged, his marriage contract of 1613, is that he was not schooled in the mainstream of Roman painting. "Maestro Baldassare," whom he named as his teacher, was undoubtedly a marginal artist, possibly Balthasar Lauwers (see Patrice Marandel's introduction). The fact is that from the first years of the Seicento onward, Roman "high art"—firmly grounded in High Renaissance, first embodied in the so-called "Maniera" of the second Mannerism in the latter part of the sixteenth century, later to form the Baroque style—had lost its absolutism. Concurrently, the contemporary art-theory which propagandized it had by then turned doctrinaire, and thus had lost its infallibility in the face of the proliferation of styles, the emergence of new movements and the acclimitization, both in Rome and in Naples, of foreign artists, ultramontane for the most part and steeped in their native traditions.

By the time of Nomé's schooling and the time of his earliest dated work, *The Martyrdom of Saint Catherine* (1617), the concept of *invenzione* that had been fundamental to art theory since the early Renaissance, and which, from Alberti to Mannerism with Vasari (1568), Lomazzo (1584), and Zuccaro (1607) combined what we mean by subject-matter and composition, had taken on a new and subjective meaning. Both the old objective meaning and the new subjective one are given their respective definitions together for the first time, it seems, and in contrast to each other, by Borghini, an otherwise unoriginal art-theoretician, by and large imitative of Vasari, in 1584.[2]

There are, then, two types of *invenzione,* according to Borghini: one which borrows from art motifs and compositions for mythological, historical, and religious scenes; and one which is literally a figment of the artist's imagination. The latter creates motifs such as costumes, scenes—including balls, weddings, hunts, and even battles—for which there may be no suitable models in art but only in the artist's fantasy *(capriccio).* The coupling of this type of *invenzione* (which turns out to be synonymous with a modern word, imagination) with *capriccio* is at the root of our understanding not only of Nomé's art, but of genre painting of the Baroque and Rococo as well as what falls between it and the "grand style," specifically artists like Salvator Rosa mentioned above by Wittkower in tribute to Nomé, or Watteau.

Several years later, in 1591, Comanini draws a similar distinction between pictorial description from nature and the representation of the fantastic that the artist sometimes is able to draw from his own imagination, "a *capriccio* of his own."[3] Thus, to both Borghini and Comanini, *capriccio* is the product of subjective invention, and it is not by chance that both notions are conjoined in the title of Piranesi's series of etchings, *Invenzioni capricciose de carceri* (1745). *Capriccio* is a key concept for the understanding of Nomé's aesthetic ambience, and the students of Nomé, including Patrice Marandel in his introduction to the present catalogue, have not failed to underscore the significance of Callot's *Capricci de varie figure* published in Florence in 1617.

Capriccio, a synonym for fantasy, is lumped together by Zuccaro in 1607 with "things heteroclite and fantastic."[4] Such inventions dictated by fancy (Borghini) thrive on the bizarre, the deformed, the horrific, the metamorphic, the cataclysmic, and the macabre, all of which is found in the art of Bosch. Besides all of this, another aspect emerges clearly from the present exhibition: Nomé's ability, by means of glittering sculptural accretions upon plausible—

rather than real—architectures and the Gothic immensity of some interiors, to conjure up the enchantment of the unreal, a sort of transfiguration—halcyon or catastrophic—which invites the viewer to penetrate the unknown through his familiarity with the outer world, as well as, inwardly, through his fantasies.

Comanini rightly understood that the irreverence inherent to *capriccio* makes it unacceptable for sacred subjects in Counter-Reformation times. Such subjects, however, are preponderant in this exhibition, yet the religious motif, far from dominating the compositions as it does in Baroque and classical painting, is characteristically inconspicuous: its role in the economy of the composition is hardly less perfunctory than the acknowledgement of religion in Descartes' *Discourse*; they are religious fables for mere aesthetic enjoyment rather than the spiritual delectation of Nomé's private patrons, and this accounts for the cabinet-picture format of so many of his paintings.

The diminutive size of the figures, the preponderance of scenography— the decor of *Heliodorus Expelled from the Temple* evokes a print for a contemporary edition of a Monteverdi opera—are equally redolent of so-called *Bambocciata,* or genre painting from the Netherlands acclimatized to Rome and eventually Naples during the third decade of the seventeenth century. The penlike frenzy of the brush inherent to *capriccio* was readily accessible to the *Bamboccianti,* and one wonders whether the many small figures which people the awesome landscape of *The Martyrdom of San Gennaro* of 1622 (North Carolina Museum of Art, Raleigh; pl. 1) are not features of *Bambocciate*, although they precede by three years the first *Bambocciata* recorded in Rome by Pieter van Laer (*The Water-Carriers,* Galleria Nazionale). Laer was himself nicknamed "Bamboccio" for his droll appearance. He and his followers specialized in this pictorial genre, well established in the Low Countries and very much at home in middle-class interiors, but new in Rome. It popularized street scenes often teeming with small personages *(Bambocci)* and rustic subjects set in briskly brushed landscapes. *Bamboccianti,* as these painters were called, is a rather pejorative sobriquet. The genre may well have reached Naples from the Low Countries concomitantly or independently from Rome at the time when Nomé entered a Neapolitan workshop.

The present exhibition is the first one to be devoted to a single old master painter at The Menil Collection. The affinity, real or assumed, between his work and Surrealism—which Marandel discusses in his introduction—has played its part in winning the admittance of the two paintings by the artist to The Menil Collection, of which Surrealist art is a major component.

Marandel had once before, in 1973, been called upon by Dominique de Menil to curate an exhibition of grisaille painting titled "Gray is the Color," which featured one of the two Nomé paintings in the collection, *A City in Ruins at Night*. His expertise with seventeenth-century and eighteenth-century painting in France and Italy and his familiarity with Neapolitan painting designated him to write this catalogue. Indeed, his grasp of the milieu—artistic, social, and geographical—has led here to new insights into Nomé's work.

The present exhibition is both ambitious and modest, the former in that it is the first retrospective given to Nomé since the great exhibition at the John and Mable Ringling Museum in Sarasota devoted to this artist in 1950, which to date remains an unsurpassed event. It is modest in that it is limited to fourteen paintings, in part for practical considerations, but more profoundly for reasons formulated in 1987 by the late Charles Sterling, a giant in the field of old European painting. His association with our collection and his solicitude on personal as well as on scholarly levels will always be vividly and gratefully remembered at the Menil. The best way to express our gratitude and to honor his memory is to give him the last word, citing his closing thoughts on Nomé's *A City in Ruins in at Night*:

> To find François de Nomé's kindred spirits, one could turn to Victor Hugo, whose powerful wash-drawings are as good as those done by professionals. De Nomé, Magnasco, and Hugo present a chiaroscuro charged with an expressive thrust approaching brutality. It is difficult to find other examples of such recurrent chiaroscuro outside that of Chinese brushwork.
>
> The effects of overemphasis carry an imminent danger. "That which is exaggerated is insignificant," said Talleyrand. . . . A gathering of more than ten works by each of these artists produces an irresistible impression of procedure and routine—the poetic emotion that inspired them being no longer credible.[5]

Bertrand Davezac
Curator
The Menil Collection

1. Rudolph Wittkower. *Art and Architecture in Italy, 1600 to 1750*. Baltimore: Penguin Books, 1958, p. 232.

2. Raffaelo Borghini. *Il riposo*. Florence: 1584, pp. 65–76. (Reprint, Milan: ed. M. Rossi, 1957.)

3. Gregorio Comanini. *Il figino*. Mantua: 1691. His distinction between "pittori icastici" and "pittori fantastici" corresponds to Borghini's distinction between the two kinds of invention. (E. Panofsky. *Idea*. Columbia: University of South Carolina Press, 1968, Appendix II, p. 253, n. 37.)

4. Federico Zuccaro. *Idea di Pittori, Scultori e Architetti*. Turin: 1607. (Reprint, *Scritti d'arte de Federico Zuccaro*. Florence: ed. D. Heikamp, 1961.)

5. Charles Sterling. "A City in Ruins at Night by François de Nomé," *The Menil Collection: A Selection from the Palaeolithic to the Modern Era*. New York: Harry N. Abrams, 1987, p. 90.

Introduction

J. Patrice Marandel

I

It is not unusual for the art historian to encounter work by artists whose identities are unknown. Many artists of the early Renaissance are recognized only through similarities among their works, patiently established by way of analogies and comparisons. Archives have not yielded information about their lives. Their existence is only evidenced in this way; as human figures, they are shadows.

"Monsù Desiderio" is a shadowy figure of another kind: the name appears to identify an artist with a distinctive oeuvre, but in fact conceals a situation of confused identities. The painter called "Monsù Desiderio" in the abundant literature of the past fifty years, the author of the extravagant paintings of ruins and church interiors associated with that name, was not one individual.

It was established almost forty years ago by Raffaelo Causa[1] that three artists hid under the name first coined by De Dominici,[2] the early historian of the Neapolitan school, in 1742: two artists from the Lorraine, François de Nomé and Didier Barra, and a third artist—anonymous for Causa—but identified as an engraver from Pistoia, Francesco Desideri. More recently yet, Jacques Thuillier has demonstrated that the name "Monsù Desiderio" should be reserved for the landscape painter Didier Barra.[3]

Born in Metz between 1590 and 1595, Barra reached a certain notoriety in Naples. De Dominici, referring to him appropriately as "Monsù Desiderio"— Monsù being the traditional appellation to designate a foreigner, Desiderio an italianization of his French name, Didier—calls him "famoso pittore di prospettive e vedute di citta." A point of reference for the reconstruction of Barra's oeuvre is a work inscribed and dated 1647, a view of Naples (Naples, Museo di San Martino) which displays Barra's original talent as a cartographic painter.[4] Barra's work remained fairly well known through the nineteenth century. G. B. Chiarini, describing in the mid-nineteenth century the large altarpiece representing San Gennaro protecting the City of Naples in the Arciconfraternita della Trinita dei Pellegrini, refers to it as a collaboration between the Neapolitan painter Onofrio Palumbo "e lo straniero detto Monsù Desiderio," credited for having painted the "prospettiva di Napoli."[5] In these sources concerning Didier Barra, alias Monsù Desiderio, nowhere is there mention of François de Nomé.

François de Nomé was also born in Metz, around 1593—a date that would make him the exact contemporary of his compatriot with whom he has been so often confused. The most compelling document to have surfaced that sheds light on the artist is his marriage contract of 1613, in which the artist made a lengthy exposition of his background.[6] At the time of his marriage, the artist claimed to have left his country eleven years earlier. He had then settled in Rome and studied with a "Maestro Baldassare," whose last name he did not remember. Causa has argued that this Maestro Baldassare may have been the little-known Flemish artist Balthasar Lauwers (whose sons Francesco and Filippo Lauri are better known), a landscape painter and a pupil of Paul Brill and Agostino Tassi.

Around 1610, François de Nomé established himself in Naples. The reasons for his move to the city are not known, but his success there is attested by the abundance of his work—itself the reflection of the active market (only one commission is, however, firmly documented, a series of canvases illustrating the story of a Pharaoh, for a certain Francesco de Maria in 1618).[7] After 1634—the latest date found on a painting—nothing is known of the artist. The year of his death is not recorded.

While modern scholarship has patiently attempted to separate the various artists designated under the same name, and restore to each their own works, it may be revealing to wonder what has led to such confusion.

Although less is known of Didier Barra's life, the similarity in the backgrounds of both artists is striking. Born perhaps the same year, in the same

Fig. 1. Didier Barra, now reattributed to François de Nomé, *A View of Naples*, n.d.
Oil on canvas, 66¼ x 69 in. (115 x 75.5 cm). Silbernagl Collection, Daverio, Italy.

town, both artists ended up in the same foreign city. Neither of them painted in what can be considered the mainstream of art at the time, large religious or historical compositions, but specialized rather in the more marginal fields of topographic views and painted architecture.[8] Nothing indicates that they apprenticed together, but to affirm, however, that Barra and Nomé did not have any contact with one another would be absurd.[9] If one accepts Causa's identification of Maestro Baldassare with Balthasar Lauwers, one cannot but be intrigued by the fact that Nomé's master left a small name in art history for having participated with others in the decoration of the "Galleria Geografica" in the Vatican. There Lauwers painted notably the Port of Ancona, in a way anticipating the very genre that insured the reputation of Didier Barra.

Nothing indicates either that the two artists shared a studio, or collaborated on paintings. Yet the occasional similarity of their works—if one accepts to a large extent the results of M. R. Nappi's recent research[10] — is troubling. *A View of Naples* (Daverio, Silbernagl coll.; fig. 1),[11] once thought to be by Barra and displaying his somber palette, has been now reattributed to Nomé by Nappi. Likewise, a painting of an imaginary building, signed by Didier Barra and dated 1647 (Modena, private collection; fig. 2),[12] is unthinkable without some awareness of the work of Nomé.

François de Nomé's reputation—or at least his name—may have fallen rapidly into oblivion. When less than a century after his death, Count Harrach—the viceroy of Naples, and an intrepid collector of Neapolitan works—purchased five paintings by him (which still remain in the Harrach collection in Schloss Rohrau, near Vienna), they were sold to him as the works of Monsù Desiderio, that is, Didier Barra. Two lessons can be drawn from this sale. First of all, that in spite of the artist's identity being lost, the works of François de Nomé were still deemed fit to enter one of the greatest collections of local artists. Secondly, that a confusion already existed between the two artists. Ignorance rather than greed on the part of the agent arranging the sale must have been the reason for the confusion (both artists are likely to have commanded relatively similar prices). Was it their foreign and common origin that led them to be lumped together, or were there more personal ties between the two artists that were still known in the early eighteenth century?

Then mystery built itself upon confusion. Out of ignorance, many writers gave currency to the invented name "Monsù Desiderio," unaware that more

Fig. 2. Didier Barra, *Imaginary Building*, n.d. Oil on canvas, 8½ x 11¼ in. (21.5 x 28.5 cm). Private collection, Modena, Italy.

than one artist was hidden behind it. Thus the identity of François de Nomé was obscured.

It is an indication of the fascination François de Nomé exerted upon the modern mind to realize the amount of books, articles, and literature in general his work has generated for the past fifty years. Never has an obscure artist, albeit original and intriguing, given rise to such a large exegesis. A myth rapidly created itself around the painter: his name was supposed to bring the *malocchio*—the evil eye—and could not be pronounced fully; owning his paintings was strictly at the collector's risk. There were rumors of fires bursting out in museums where his works were kept, of accidents happening to scholars studying his work or photographers at work on his paintings. A malefic, but tantalizing, aura emanated from the work.

Coincidentally, the early publication in 1935 by the French art historian Louis Réau of the Harrach paintings took place at a time when the Surrealists, backed up by Freudian analysis, were exploring in literature as in the visual arts those manifestations which they considered to be their precedents. This interest in François de Nomé had its positive aspect: paintings long ignored or relegated to the obscure recesses of small museums were brought to light again. Critical appreciation of the work developed, however, in three directions: that of "L'art fantastique," illustrated for instance in Marcel Brion's book on the subject published in 1961—an anthology of the rare and the bizarre which included Nomé's architectural fantasies as well as Victor Hugo's drawings; the poetic and psychoanalytic approach exemplified by the numerous publications on the artist by Dr. Felix Sluys, an approach that found in the painter's creations the expression of an existential malaise—the ruins being a metaphor for man's destitution.

The third direction developed less successfully, being perhaps closer to the truth. In 1950, the Sarasota Museum under the direction of A. Everett Austin, Jr. consecrated Nomé—then still called Monsù Desiderio—with a large monographic exhibition. Nomé's work intersected with two main interests of the enlightened museum director: his love and understanding of the Baroque, and his predilection for the theater.[13] Nomé's artificially lit, stagelike compositions could in many ways prefigure the decorative and mildly surrealistic sets of Eugene Berman, an artist friend of Austin whom he admired and collected.

These three approaches contributed greatly to the fame of Nomé in our century. Never had an old master seemed to prefigure to such extent the preoccupations and aesthetic choices of another generation. In 1966, when Thomas Hess, then editor of *Art News,* published a group of articles under the title *The Grand Eccentrics,* [14] the illustration chosen for the cover was a detail of Nomé's *Explosion in a Church* (pl. 13). Although, in his introduction, Hess did not dwell at length on the artist, and in spite of the fact that none of the following essays was devoted to him, Nomé had come to personify by then the eccentric artist par excellence.

II

To this day, Nomé's works upset our preconceived ideas of what classical painting should be. How could a contemporary of Poussin not echo the ideals of seventeenth-century classicism? Why this insistence on effects? Why this willing rejection of order and calm? Why would an artist of that time eschew, in a word, the dignity that seems to qualify all his contemporaries?

A basis for answering these questions could be found in the eccentricity of the artist. By this, we do not mean his psychological unbalance, imagined by some writers, but more literally his geographic eccentricity. Our century, prisoner of its own frontiers, has imposed upon us a vision of the past as centralized as is today's world. In France in particular, the great effort of unification and centralization of the country begun by Cardinal Richelieu, Louis XIII's powerful minister, and achieved under Louis XIV, has been responsible for making us forget the prodigious cultural diversity among regional centers, just prior to this politics of centralization. Politically independent, the Duchy of Lorraine, on one hand, is tied culturally to the Kingdom of France, with which it shares its language. [15] On the other, its location between France and the German empire is responsible for some affinities with the latter, [16] as well as for the development of an axis with the Italian peninsula, where the majority of artists from Lorraine studied and worked.

François de Nomé's life did not escape that tradition. In his own words, he left his country at the age of nine *"con altre persone."* Who were these other persons? Must one think of his entire family "relocating" in Italy for some unknown reason? Or did the young boy succumb at that early age to the appeal of Italy? Some of his compatriots did. Jacques Callot allegedly joined a troupe of Bohemians at the age of twelve, moved by the desire to see "the beautiful things" he had already heard were to be found in Italy, and Claude Lorrain (pseudonym of Claude Gellée) was in Rome by the age of thirteen. So little is known of Nomé's life that one is often reduced to conjectures, but enough is known of the pattern young foreign artists followed upon arrival in Rome to eliminate from his life all romanticization.

Whatever the circumstances of his coming to Rome, he rapidly entered the studio of "Maestro Baldassare," already identified here—although somewhat hypothetically—as Balthasar Lauwers. It has been now established that if this is the case, Lauwers could have been Nomé's first and only master,[17] but more importantly yet, it must be noticed that Lauwers was married to the daughter of Henry Cousin, a goldsmith whose more famous relatives included the two painters of the School of Fontainebleau, both named Jean Cousin, the elder being himself the author of a Treaty of Prospective.[18] The same Lauwers may also have introduced Nomé to the work of H. Vredeman de Vries, whose own Treaty of Prospective was published in 1604–1605.

The foregoing account should dissipate once and for all the image of Nomé as an "eccentric" artist working in a cultural vacuum. Nomé's paintings of interiors belong to a well-defined genre that developed precisely at the time of his formative years. What must be stressed is the eccentricity not of the artist, but that of the milieu in which he was formed. In Rome, his teacher was a Flemish artist, married to a French woman; the examples from which he seemingly derived his style were equally "foreign"—the School of Fontainebleau, perhaps, and Vredeman de Vries, another Flemish artist whose paintings of church interiors were particularly appreciated at the court of Rudolf II in Prague.

Not different in this respect from many other foreign artists who, from the sixteenth to the nineteenth century, gathered in Rome, the artists from Lorraine seemed to have formed in the seventeenth century a coherent group.[19] Although it is likely that Nomé was part of this group, only a few documents can prove it. One of the witnesses at his wedding was "Nicola Romeo di

Fig. 3. Ligier Richier's sculptures for the Monument of René Chalons at Bar-le-Duc.

Fig. 4. Jacques Callot, *The Martyrdom of Saint Sebastian*, 1621. Etching,
6½ x 12⅞ in. (16.5 x 33 cm). Rhode Island School of Design, Museum of Art.

Lorena," who stated that he had known the artist since his early days in Rome[20] (another witness was the German painter Thoman von Hagelstein, a pupil and imitator of Elsheimer). As we have already mentioned, the confusion made with his compatriot Didier Barra may allude to a certain intimacy between the two artists. Given the absence of documents, it is even more intriguing that M. R. Nappi has astutely noticed many instances in which the artist quotes in his own paintings from other artists of the Lorraine.

These include, in particular, Nicolas Cordier, one of the most important sculptors in Rome at the turn of the century. A direct contact between the two artists is not to be excluded, and it is probably Cordier who reminded Nomé of (or introduced him to) the work of another Lorraine sculptor, Ligier Richier. Richier's apocalyptic world, for instance in the sculptures for the Monument of René de Chalons at Bar-le-Duc (fig. 3), provides an eloquent antecedent to some of Nomé's most ambitious compositions. Separated from the original visual sources of his native Lorraine, it is, however, remarkable to witness how Nomé was able to retain, in the middle of Rome, his cultural identity. It is also obvious that Nomé was aware of the work of Jacques Callot, the most famous artist from Lorraine active in Italy beside Claude Gellée. Again, direct contacts between the two artists are conjectural, but it suffices to compare

Nomé's *The Martyrdom of San Gennaro* (pl. 1) with Callot's *The Martyrdom of Saint Sebastian* (fig. 4) to realize the close affinity between the two artists.

Carried to an extreme, such study of Nomé's cultural milieu might lead to the erroneous image of an artist living and working in a foreign ghetto, unaware of his surroundings. Yet, whatever the motivations or reasons for Nomé's move to Italy, it is certain that there the artist was aware of "the beautiful things" that Callot had set out to see. Nomé's work is rich not only with the imported culture of his homeland, but also with a keen appreciation of his immediate surroundings. If many of his church interiors recall Northern late-Gothic buildings, most of his architecture also reflects his Italian environment. Nomé moved to Rome at a time of vigorous architectural activity. Monuments and statues were exhumed daily. Some fifty years earlier, the vision of this newly revealed past had already fired the imagination of the great French poet Joachim du Bellay. Nomé's images of decaying buildings have often been compared to the sonnets which make up Du Bellay's "Antiquitez de Rome"—reflections on time passing and human frailty—but such parallelism can only be established to the detriment of both artist and poet. Yet the visual and emotional power of freshly excavated monuments, indeed of an entire antique city coming back to life—as a ruin—must be taken into account to understand the general climate in which Nomé's work developed.

III

In spite of the riches Rome could provide the young painter, it was in another city, Naples, that he established himself. It is there too that his trace is lost. Did he ever return to Rome, or to his native Lorraine? Thus far no document has been found that allows us to even consider this possibility.

The reasons for his move to the meridional city are, again, purely conjectural. According to his marriage contract, he must have arrived in Naples in 1610, exactly a year after his friend and fellow painter Thoman von Hagelstein had settled there. The choice of Naples was not an obvious one. The city was lively, in full development, and its port conferred on it an international flavor. Yet, compared to Rome, there were far fewer foreign artists. Besides François de Nomé, hardly any artists from the Lorraine can be accounted there, if one makes the exception of Claude Gellée who remained intermittently in Naples for a total of perhaps two years between 1618 and 1622 in order to study with the German painter Gottfried Wals.

However, through his Flemish contacts in Rome, Nomé may have been introduced to the active community of Flemish painters, led by Dirck Hendricksz, that flourished in the city. Hendricksz did in fact most likely collaborate with Loys Croys, whose daughter Isabella married Nomé in 1613. Altogether, Naples may have provided a more inviting enviroment to Nomé than Rome. He may have had the intelligence to realize that his compositions in spite—or because—of their originality, could not compete with the new art that was being formulated by Caravaggio and the Carracci, and that to those painters was reserved the patronage of the Church and of the aristocracy.

In Naples, and especially with the support of the Flemish artists established there, Nomé could conquer a broader market, made of less official—and ultimately less demanding—clients than those he would have to satisfy in Rome. It is a pity in that respect not to know more about the primary destination of his paintings. One thing seems certain: in spite of their religious subjects, they were never intended to hang in churches and must have been intended rather for a private clientele. Was this a predominantly Neapolitan one, or were foreign clients—like Count Harrach a century later—already attracted to these compositions? Our knowledge of the history of collections in Naples, although greatly advanced by recent research, has not yet yielded the answers to such questions. [21]

In any case, foreign artists in seventeenth-century Naples seem to have answered a growing demand for paintings of a certain type which local artists were unable or unwilling to provide. Nomé's marginal position in the general scheme of seventeenth-century Italian art becomes more relative once the particular milieu in which he appears to have moved in Naples is taken into consideration. Flemish artists were particularly famous in Naples—but also in other cities—for three types of painting: landscape, architecture, and renditions of fantastic night scenes, including in particular images of Hell. Nomé, who through his master Lauwers had been acquainted with the landscapes of Paul Brill, for the most part relinquished this aspect of the Northern tradition—although *The Martyrdom of San Gennaro* in this exhibition (pl. 1) is a counterexample—and concentrated on the other two.

In relation to his work it is essential to consider the creations of two artists active in Naples at the time of Nomé: Jakob Isaac Swanenburgh and Filippo d'Angeli (or de Llano)—better known as Filippo Napoletano. It is difficult to establish the exact links that may have united the three painters. Yet their works, and certain aspects of their life, indicate that they could not have been strangers to one another.

Filippo Napoletano was probably born in Naples of Spanish parents, but his career developed in his native city in the circle of Gottfried Wals, the German painter with whom Claude Gellée studied. He left Naples shortly after Nomé settled there, leaving, as it were, his position as a painter of nocturnal scenes to the newcomer. Curiously, Filippo Napoletano—after passing through Rome where he came into contact with Paul Brill—ended up at the court of the Grand Duke in Florence where he collaborated with another artist from Lorraine, Jacques Callot. Filippo Napoletano's repertoire prefigures and echoes in many respects that of Nomé. Both artists share a fascination for nocturnal and occasionally brutal scenes, ignited by accidental fires (naturally, it is in Naples, in the shadow of Vesuvius accompanied by the tremors of earthquakes, that such images should develop).

The same could be said of Jakob Isaac Swanenburgh, a painter born in Leiden but active in Naples between 1599 and 1617, whose subjects also include representations of witchcraft and Hell—bringing into the early seventeenth-century the kind of images of death, damnation, and Hell that painters like Hieronymous Bosch had established in Flanders a century earlier.

For Swanenburgh, "playing with fire" became literally more than representing it. In 1608, he was denounced to the Inquisition for having painted an image of witchcraft.[22] The fact is rare enough to make us wonder just how seriously their contemporaries took the kind of paintings Swanenburgh, or Nomé—the author of a majestic representation of Hell (Besançon, Musée des Beaux-Arts, fig. 5)—executed with a certain frequency.

As opposed to Rome, the center of orthodoxy, Naples always retained in its popular culture (which permeated the upper classes) a substratum of paganism. This took the form of superstitions, of a fascination with esoterica

Fig. 5. François de Nomé, *Hell*, n.d. Oil on canvas, 44½ x 68⅞ in. (113 x 175 cm). Musée des Beaux-Arts, Besançon.

and with the practice of witchcraft.[23] Although we have no proof of an active part played by the visual arts in such rituals, it is certain that they responded to this current of fashion. Trompe-l'oeil, visual tricks, unexpected textures, were commonly used by the artist to trigger in the spectator the kind of thrill theatrical seances provoked.

A well-known example of this in Naples occurred in the next century with the trick sculptures commissioned by Raimondo di Sangro—scientist, antiquarian, and charlatan—for the Chapel of Sansevero in his family palace. In Rudolfinian Prague, where the court was addicted to witchcraft (as opposed to Naples where the passion for it emanated from the people), the paintings of Arcimboldo, still-lifes and portraits at once, belong to the same aesthetics. In Nomé's case, even more than his subjects, which belong to a well-established genre, his unusual technique of thick impasto [24]—looking on close-up inspection like drippings from a candle—may indicate an intellectual game to blur the boundaries of reality and of its representation in a way akin to the alchemists' and witches' belief in the power of making things appear from nothing.

This, in any case, would only be one of the many refined aspects of Nomé's works. Again, the primary destination of his works, if known, would perhaps yield the secret of the artist. For not only his unusual technique plays tricks on us, but the general aspect of his paintings deceives. Paintings of architecture? Yes, but each tells a story, a little-known anecdote from the Old Testament, the martyrdom of a saint, the destruction of pagan idols. Many attempts have been made to interpret these paintings, their subjects and technique, as the fragments of a lonesome and isolated personality. But are they not rather evidence of the ruins of a great, complex, and esoteric culture, that of Naples in the seventeenth century, that only today patient efforts are made to retrieve from its obscurity?

1. Raffaelo Causa. "Francesco di Nome detto Monsù Desiderio." *Paragone*, 1956, no. 75, pp. 30-46.

2. B. de Dominici. *Vite dei Pittori, scultori et architetti Napoletani non mai date alla luce da autore alcuno.* Naples: Riccardi, 1742, vol. 1, p. 313.

3. Jacques Thuillier, "Un 'champ de gouilles' de l'histoire de l'art: la peinture lorraine du XVIIe siècle," in *Claude Lorrain e i pittori lorenesi in Italia nel XVII secolo*. Rome: Accademia di Francia a Roma, 1982, pp. 27-36.

4. Maria Rosaria Nappi, *François de Nomé e Didier Barra, L'enigma Monsù Desiderio*. Milan, Rome: Jandi Sapi Editori, 1991, p. 238 (ill.).

5. G. B. Chiarini, "Aggiunzoni," in *Notizie del Bello, dell'Antico et del Curioso della città di Napoli*, ed. C. Celano, vol. 4. Naples: Stamperia Nicola Mencaglia, 1856–1860, p. 809.

6. See Causa, *op. cit.*, p. 33.

7. See Causa, *op. cit.*, p. 32.

8. There is some evidence that François de Nomé somewhat broadened his field and included at least still-lifes in his repertoire. See for instance Jean-Claude Lebensztejn, "Une Vanité de Monsù Desiderio," *L'Oeil*, 1967, no. 156, pp. 2–9.

9. In spite of recent vigorous scholarly efforts, the study of the milieu of the painters of Lorraine established in Rome in the seventeenth century has still much to yield.

10. See Nappi, *op. cit.*

11. See Nappi, *op. cit.*, p. 103, no. A 47 (ill.).

12. See Nappi, *op. cit.*, p. 237, no. C 15 (ill.).

13. See *A. Everett Austin, Jr., A Director's taste and achievements*; foreword by Sir Osbert Sitwell; preface by C. C. Cunningham and K. Donahue. Sarasota: The John and Mable Ringling Museum, 1958.

14. Art News Annual, *The Grand Eccentrics*, ed. Thomas B. Hess. New York: Newsweek, Inc., 1966.

15. On the importance of this linguisitic community, see Thuillier, *op. cit.*

16. Paintings by another artist from Lorraine, Jacques Bellange, have been sometimes mistakenly attributed to Hans von Aachen. The international nature of Bellange's style

has been briefly discussed by Pierre Rosenberg in *De Nicolo dell'Abate à Nicolas Poussin: aux sources du Classicisme, 1550–1650*; Meaux: Musée Bossuet, n.d. [1989].

17. See Nappi, *op. cit.*, 1991, p. 8.

18. See *L'Ecole de Fontainebleau.* Paris: Réunion des Musées Nationaux, 1972, no. 679, p. 464.

19. See Thuillier, *op. cit.*, pp. 30–32.

20. See Causa, *op. cit.*, p. 33; also Nappi, *op. cit.*, p. 325.

21. See in particular Renata Ruotolo, "Aspetti del collezionismo napoletano del '600," in *Civiltà del Seicento a Napoli,* vol. 1, pp. 44–48. Naples: Soprintendenza dei beni Culturali, 1984.

22. See Nappi, *op. cit.*, pp. 25–26.

23. See Biagio De Giovanni, "Magia e scienza nella Napoli seicentesca," in *Civiltà del Seicento a Napoli,* vol. I. Naples: Soprintendenza dei beni Culturali, 1984, pp. 29–40.

24. See M. R. Nappi's comparison of Nomé's technique with Angelo Caroselli's technique of painting fabrics in his *Vanitas* pictures, *op. cit.*, pp. 30–31.

Catalogue of the Exhibition

1. *The Martyrdom of San Gennaro [Saint Januarius],* 1622
oil on canvas
30 x 40 in.   (76.2 x 101.6 cm)
North Carolina Museum of Art, Raleigh
Purchased with funds from the State of North Carolina

San Gennaro, patron saint and protector of Naples, was the subject of particular devotion in his city. Representations of his martyrdom abound in Neapolitan art, and Nomé himself approached the subject on several occasions. This painting is contemporaneous with the construction of the Chapel of San Gennaro, designed by Francesco Grimaldi, and erected between 1608 and 1637 in the Naples Duomo.

The canvas strikes a different note in Nomé's oeuvre: although the somber light is consistent with the gravity of the subject and with Nomé's palette, the setting in a vast landscape, the relatively modest part played by the ruins, and the proliferation of scattered figures are unusual for the artist. — J. P. M.

Inscriptions: On the triumphal arch: DO K R / 1622

Provenance: [Julius Weitzner, New York and London]
acquired by the museum in 1952

Exhibitions: New York, 1963–1964, no. 2
Houston, 1964, no. 9

Literature: Valentiner, 1956, no. 183
Bier, 1961
Sluys, 1961, no. 39
The Queens College Art Collection, 1963, no. 2 (ill.)
Rosenberg, 1982, p. 367, no. 12 (ill.)
Bowron, 1983, p. 144 (ill.)
Wright, 1985, p. 176
Nappi, 1991, p. 159, no. A 83 (ill.)

2. *The Destruction by Fire of Sodom and Gomorrah*, n.d.
oil on panel
16⅜ x 35½ in. (41.6 x 90.1 cm)
Musée des Beaux-Arts, Montreal

This painting has been known since the mid-nineteenth century, and has always been attributed to Monsù Desiderio/François de Nomé. In their 1972 census of Italian paintings in North American collections, Federico Zeri and Burton Fredericksen have followed the traditional attribution to Nomé, while questioning it. Maria Rosaria Nappi rejects the attribution. The presence of this painting in the exhibition can, however, be justified by its exceptional quality. Furthermore, the painting shows a close dependence —notably in the architecture—upon François de Nomé's work, thus opening up the difficult question of the existence of a *bottega* and of collaborators around the artist. The importance devoted to the landscape in the foreground is, indeed, atypical of Nomé's work and could suggest, as advanced by Nappi, the hand of a Flemish artist. By training, Nomé had been close to Flemish painters, and it is possible that his work found admirers and followers among the community of northern artists established in Naples. — J. P. M.

Provenance: Wallarf Collection, Cologne (in 1863)
Dr. Gottschewsky, Hamburg
Dr. Kurt Erasmus, Berlin
[Durlacher Bros., New York, in 1961]
given to the Museum of Fine Arts, Montreal (1962)
    by H. and A. Townsend

Exhibitions: Sarasota, 1950, no. 4
New York, 1961, "Juxtapositions," Durlacher Brothers,
    (Jan. 31–Feb. 15, 1961)
Houston, 1961, "Festival of the Bible in the Arts"
    Houston, Temple Emanuel (Mar. 11–26, 1961)

Literature: Parthey, 1863, I, p. 321
Sobotka, 1913, VII, p. 131
Réau, 1935, I, p. 249
Ringling Museum, 1950, p. 36, pl. 7 (ill.)
Sluys, 1961, p. 108, n. 86
Houston, 1961 (ill.)
Fredericksen and Zeri, 1972, p. 151
Nappi, 1991, p. 299, no. D 54 (ill., not by Nomé)

3. *Imaginary Architecture with Ruins and a Sarcophagus,* 1624
oil on canvas
18⅜ x 27⅝ in.   (46.5 x 70 cm)
Musée des Arts Décoratifs, Paris

This painting is a pendant of *The Flight into Egypt* (pl. 4), also dated 1624. Like the latter, it is primarily a representation of Gothic buildings, of the kind Nomé may have known in Lorraine. Like *The Flight into Egypt* also, a roundel on the central building bears a classical motif, in this case a depiction of Hercules fighting the Nemean Lion. A composition that is practically devoid of figures, the presence of a half-buried sarcophagus and buildings more destroyed than ruined, altogether conjure up an image of war and devastation. Could one, without pressing the point too far, establish a link between such a desolate image and the plight of Nomé's native Lorraine during the Thirty Years War (1618–1648)? In 1622, the army of Mansfeld had crossed Lorraine and devastated the country, committing atrocities. — J. P. M.

Inscriptions: Over the central arch of the villa: 1624

Provenance: E. Peyre collection

Literature: Pariset, 1952, pp. 261–264
Brion, 1954, pp. 2 and 6
Causa, 1956, p. 43
Sluys, 1961, p. 119, no. 98 (ill.)
Seghers, 1981, pp. 89, 91 (ill.)
Nappi, 1991, p. 197, no. A 117 (ill.)

4. *The Flight into Egypt,* 1624

oil on canvas

18⅜ x 27⅝ in. (46.5 x 70 cm)

Musée des Arts Décoratifs, Paris

The representation of the Holy Family's Flight into Egypt, in the foreground, is dwarfed by an imposing and fantastic architecture—made even more unreal by the artist's use of monochromatic tones and artificial lighting—which constitutes the real subject matter of the painting. This minimization of the nominal subject matter in order to enhance its context is common in the painting of the time, and can be found in particular in the works of Claude Gellée, an artist who—through his roots in Lorraine—shares a common cultural background with Nomé.

In her recent monograph on the artist, Maria Rosaria Nappi has pointed out some of the elements which in this painting betray the wide and varied culture of Nomé, in particular the representation on the right part of the church of a centaur in a roundel—a theme borrowed from the Antique, but perhaps even more directly from Raphael—and of a Pietà, a theme commonly used in Neapolitan churches. — J. P. M.

Inscriptions: On the wall under the windows on the right side of the cathedral: 1624

Provenance: E. Peyre Collection

Exhibitions: Saarbrück & Rouen, 1954, no. 64
Bordeaux, 1957, pp. 17–18, no. 43

Literature: Pariset, 1952, pp. 251-264
Causa, 1956, p. 43
Brion, 1961 (ill.)
Sluys, 1961, p. 99, n. 73 (ill.)
Lebensztejn, 1967, fig. 9 (ill.)
Seghers, 1981, p. 43 (ill.)
Nappi, 1991, pp. 198–199, no. A 118 (ill.)

5. *The Flight into Egypt*, n.d.
oil on canvas
32¼ x 51¼ in. (82.6 x 130.2 cm)
The Museum of Fine Arts, Houston

This painting probably is to be dated rather early in Nomé's career. In contrast with the painting of the same subject in the Musée des Arts Décoratifs, Paris (pl. 4), this canvas presents elements which one hesitates to call naturalistic, but which betray in any case Nomé's awareness of landscape painting and his training among Flemish painters from the circle of Paul Brill. The figures in this composition are by another hand, probably that of Belisario Corenzio, an artist whom B. de Dominici, in his *Vite dei pittori, scultori ed architetti Napoletani,* published in 1743, and who was said to have collaborated with "Monsù Desiderio." — J. P. M.

Provenance: [Christie's, London, 1941]
[Durlacher Bros., New York]
Samuel H. Kress Collection, 1948

Exhibitions: Sarasota, 1950, no. 67

Literature: Ringling Museum, 1950, p. 22 (ill.)
Sluys, 1957
Sluys, 1961, p. 82, no. 49 (ill.)
Fredericksen and Zeri, 1972, p. 151
Nappi, 1991, p. 151, no. A 80 (ill.)

6. *The Head of St. John the Baptist Being Presented to Salome*, n.d.
oil on copper
7½ x 9½ in. (18.9 x 24 cm)
The Walters Art Gallery, Baltimore

This painting is a pendant of the one following (pl. 7), and displays even more vehemently Nomé's *"cuir repoussé"* technique. Drawing from a different source than for its pendant, Nomé has based his composition upon an actual monument of Rome, the Column of Marcus-Antonius, now in the center of Piazza Colonna. The building on the right could even be loosely based on an antique monument that still existed during Nomé's sojourn in Rome, the Basilica of Antonius Pius. The disposition of the Piazza, as it appeared some years before Nomé's arrival in Rome, can be seen in an engraving by Du Perac in his *Vestigi dell'antichità di Roma raccolti in perspettiva,* published in Rome in 1575, which on this evidence may have been known to Nomé. The indication on the engraving's legend that the basilica was originally adorned with forty-two columns may have also contributed to firing Nomé's imagination in reconstructing this antique building, to which he gave a fantastic appearance.
— J. P. M.

Inscriptions: In lower center: S.MATT.CAP.XIIII [Matthew 14]

Provenance: Don Marcello Massarenti, Rome
acquired by the museum in 1902

Exhibitions: Sarasota, 1950, no. 2
New York, 1962, no. 2
New York 1967, no. 18

Literature: H. Walters, 1909, 1922, 1929, no. 329
Ringling Museum, p. 16, no. 2, pl. xxiv (ill.)
Sluys, 1961, p. 76, no. 42
Gabhart, 1969, no. 22 (ill.)
Fredericksen and Zeri, 1972, p. 151
Zeri, 1976, vol. II, p. 466, no. 343 (ill.)
Nappi, 1991, pp. 78–79, no. A 27 (ill.)

7. *St. Paul Preaching to the Athenians*, n.d.
oil on copper
7½ x 9½ in. (18.9 x 24 cm)
The Walters Art Gallery, Baltimore

This representation is based upon a well-known composition on the same subject by Raphael, executed in tapestry. It is possible that Nomé had knowledge only of the engraving after it by Marcantonio Raimondi, although the fact that Nomé's composition is in reverse of the engraving seems to indicate that he may have had the possibility of copying it directly.

Particularly typical of a certain group of pictures by Nomé is the peculiar technique evidenced here of *"cuir repoussé,"* which consists in working a rather thick impasto with a tool such as the tip of the brush. Scholars such as Jacques Thuillier and Federico Zeri have associated this technique with the maturity of the artist. — J. P. M.

Inscriptions: Lower right corner: ACTI.CAP.XVII [Acts 17]

Provenance: Don Marcello Massarenti, Rome
acquired by the museum in 1902

Exhibitions: Sarasota, 1950, no. 1
New York, 1962, no. 1
New York 1967, no. 17

Literature: H. Walters, 1909, 1922, 1929, no. 329
Ringling Museum, no. 1, pl. xxiii (ill.)
Sluys, 1961, p. 76, no. 41 (ill.)
Fredericksen and Zeri, 1972, p. 151
Zeri, 1976, vol. II, p. 466, no. 342
Nappi, 1991, p. 76, no. A 26 (ill.)

8. *The Burning of Troy and the Flight of Aeneas*, n.d.
oil on canvas
45⅝ x 71⅞ in. (116 x 182.5 cm)
Nationalmuseum, Stockholm

For all its classical references, in subject matter as well as in borrowed motifs, this representation of the Burning of Troy eschews the classical dignity that characterizes many of its depictions by other artists. Here human figures and the architecture (obviously both painted in this case by Nomé himself, who occasionally left the painting of his figures to other artists) are painted uniformly. Both their texture and colors are similar. In spite— or because—of this lack of realism, Nomé achieves an image of apocalyptic dimension that rings true, akin in spirit to the very realistic descriptions of war by Nomé's fellow countryman, Jacques Callot.

Pontus Grate has deciphered an almost illegible date on the painting as 1623, arguing also a similarity between the Stockholm picture and the painting of Hell in Besançon (fig. 5, Introduction), which is dated 1622. One could also point out a similarity between the imaginary sculpture group on a stele at the right in the Stockholm composition and the one at the right in *The Flight into Egypt* (Paris, Musée des Arts Décoratifs [pl. 4]) dated 1624, to confirm a date in the very early years of the century's third decade. — J. P. M.

Provenance: [Christie's, London, April 3, 1987, no. 78]
[Colnaghi's, London]
acquired by the museum in 1987

Exhibitions: Stockholm, 1986, no. 23

Literature: P. Grate, 1988, pp. 52–3, pl. 23 (ill.)
Nappi, 1991, p. 176, no. A 97 (ill.)

9. *The Circumcision in the Temple,* 1623
oil on canvas
47¼ x 58⅜ in. (121.3 x 148.3 cm)
Yale University Art Gallery, New Haven
Leonard C. Hanna, Jr. B.A. 1913, Fund

Nothing is known of the early history of this painting, yet its highly accomplished composition, which also displays a degree of technical perfection seldom attained by the artist, suggests that it had been executed for an important and exacting patron. The scene departs from the usual representations of The Circumcision, not so much in the depiction of the circumcision itself (although the processional cortege of attendants pulling a sacrificial bull—a theme Nomé employed in other compositions—is rare), as in its unusual setting. Nomé has chosen to represent this circumcision in a "space" that is both indoors and outdoors—or neither—and resembles, in fact, a truncated architectural model. Strong lighting effects reinforce the artificiality of the setting, while playing a dynamic part in animating the canvas. Limiting his palette—even in such an accomplished work—Nomé uses chiaroscuro effects, as he often does, to replace a brilliant display of colors.
— J.P.M.

Inscriptions: Signed and dated, l.r.: FRANCISCO DID NOME 1623

Provenance: Countess Manvers, North Allerton, Yorkshire
Rayner McCormal, New York
[Kleinberger, New York, 1955]
acquired by the Yale University Art Gallery in 1960

Exhibitions: "Paintings, Drawings and Sculpture from the Yale University
Art Gallery," Fogg Art Museum, Harvard University,
Oct. 5–Nov. 14, 1967
Paris-New York-Chicago, 1982, no. 77

Literature: Causa, 1956, p. 31 & 44, note 3, plate 23a & 23b
Sluys, 1961, pp. 70–71, no. 35
Kelder, 1963, p. n.
Fredericksen and Zeri, 1972, p. 151
Rosenberg, 1982, pp. 295–296, no. 77 (ill.)
Nappi 1991, p. 194, no. A 114 (ill.)

10. *Interior of a Church*, n.d.
oil on canvas
25⅛ x 50 in. (64 x 127 cm)
Museum of Fine Arts, Budapest

This imposing painting, which should be compared with the *Interior of a Cathedral* from The Menil Collection (pl. 11), presents also some of the typical ambiguities which contribute to the fascination of Nomé's work. As in the Yale *Circumcision* (pl. 9), it would be vain to attempt a definition of the space Nomé represented. The artist's imaginative use of light helps him to establish not only light and dark areas, but also to create a certain ambiguity between what is inside and what may be outside the church. For instance, the opening at the center of the composition—at the logical placement of the church's portal—leads onto another building, perhaps another church, brilliantly lit, behind which another nave seems to open. But seen differently, this golden building could be understood as an elaborate altar at the end of a nave.

The contrast between the Gothic architecture and the Renaissance monuments at the right may also indicate an awareness on the part of the artist of the changes that occurred in the design and decoration of churches at the time of his activity in Naples. Churches were then constantly being remodeled, or added to, and there was a general disappearance of Gothic architecture under Renaissance Mannerist and early Baroque ornamentation. Nomé's paintings can also be seen as an illustration of this moment in the history of taste and architecture. — J. P. M.

Provenance: Esterhazy collection, Budapest
acquired by museum in 1871

Exhibitions: Sarasota, 1950, no. 5
Nice, 1982, no. 112

Literature: Parthey, 1863, I, p. 321 Maltese, 1956, p. 67 (ill.)
Sobotka, 1913, VII, p. 131 Sluys, 1956, pp. 53–63
Van Terey, 1910, p. 224 Sluys, 1961, p. 69, no. 33
Réau, 1935 (ill.) Preiss, 1973 (ill.)
Romdahl, 1944, p. 6 Nappi, 1991, p. 177, no. A 98 (ill.)
Ringling Museum, 1950, p. 17 (ill.)

11. *Interior of a Cathedral*, n.d.
oil on canvas
76 x 124 in. (193 x 315 cm)
The Menil Collection, Houston

Both this composition and the church interior from the Budapest museum (pl. 10) first appear deceivingly simple in comparison to the majority of Nomé's paintings. In both paintings, a strict axis replaces the chaotic compositions the artist often favors. Such organized symmetry should not, however, lead the viewer to the rapid conclusion that these paintings represent another—more sedate—aspect of the artist's production. At closer inspection, the Houston painting reveals that within this apparently rigid frame the artist introduces a variety of contrasts which give the work its originality. For instance, Nomé pits details executed with particular care (e.g., the exacting rendition of the stained-glass windows, rare in Nomé's oeuvre) against broader, more "painterly" passages (such as the sculptures under the church's arches). Dark and light areas are also strongly defined, as are the figures silhouetted against the luminous background of the nave. Thus Nomé creates an optical game emanating a certain strangeness, proving in this way that he does not need the recourse of obvious oddities to establish in his painting a different climate. Likewise, this painting would indicate that Nomé's clients and patrons did not always seek the master's easiest effects, but would also look to his work for intellectual refinement. — J. P. M.

Provenance: [Victor Spark, New York, in 1950]
[Julius Weitzner, New York, in 1957]
[Wildenstein, New York, until 1960]
acquired by The Menil Collection in 1960

Exhibitions; Sarasota, 1950, no. 42
Houston, 1961
Dallas, 1961
Houston 1971–1972
Paris-New York-Chicago, 1982, no. 76

Literature: Ringling Museum, 1950, p. 34, pl. V (ill.)
Sluys, 1957, p. 69
Sluys, 1961, p. 66, no. 29 (ill.)
Rosenberg, p. 126 (ill.)
Nappi, 1991, p. 179, no. A 99 (ill.)

12. *Heliodorus Expelled from the Temple*, n.d.
oil on canvas
35½ x 56½ in. (90 x 143.5 cm)
Private collection, France

This exhibition gives us the opportunity to present a painting unknown to previous historians of Nomé. Its bright and brilliant colors are unusual for an artist whose chiaroscuro compositions established his fame, but Nomé nevertheless executed light and bright canvases, for instance a *Church Interior* in the Harrach'sche collection in Schloss Rohrau (Nappi, p. 173, A94). *Heliodorus* also shares similarities of details and color with two other Nomé paintings: *Christ and the Paralytic* (Nappi, p. 187, A107) and *Death of Ananias* (Nappi, p. 203, A121).

The subject of the Expulsion of Heliodorus—which another hand may have painted on this canvas—may have been inspired by Raphael's famous fresco at the Vatican, from which it differs, however, considerably. It should be noted that this subject encountered a certain success in Naples, where one of its most powerful interpretations was painted in 1725 by Francesco Solimena for the entrance wall of the Gesù Nuovo. — J. P. M.

Provenance: In the family of the present owner since the 18th century

Literature: Previously unpublished

13. *Asa Destroying the Statue of Priapus (Explosion in a Church)*, n.d.
oil on canvas
29⅛ x 39½ 7 in. (74 x 100.5 cm)
Fitzwilliam Museum, Cambridge

In this famous painting, often referred to as "Explosion in a Church," Nomé has represented, in fact, a little-known episode in 1 Kings 15: 11-15, identified in the inscription in the upper left corner. Asa, king of Israel, is credited with having reestablished the Judaic faith after a lapse of his people into paganism, which Asa's own mother had perpetuated. According to the Book, the destruction of the pagan idol took place on the banks of the Cedron, but Nomé placed the event in a churchlike temple, giving it a dramatic dimension that allowed him a spectacular display of characteristic effects.

It would be tempting to see in this dramatization of the subject a direct relation with the theater—whether with the secular world of the opera, a new art form at the time Nomé painted this work, or with the religious theater the Jesuits were beginning to promote in their establishments. Such interpretation must remain, however, entirely conjectural. — J. P. M.

Inscriptions:	Top left: 3 DE RE.CAP.XV [1 Kings 15]
Provenance:	Sir James Meck (d. 1856)
	R. E. A. Wilson, London
	Francis F. Madan, London
	given by him to the museum in 1962
Exhibitions:	Sarasota, 1950, no. 21
	Zurich, 1956, no. 193
	Nice, 1982
Literature:	Ringling Museum, 1950, p. 35, no. 21, pl. vi (ill.)
	Sluys, 1956, pp. 53–63
	Zurich Kunsthaus, 1956, pl. 30 (ill.)
	Sluys, 1957, p. 73
	C. Roy, 1960, p. 44
	Sluys, 1961, p. 108, no. 85 (ill.)
	P. Seghers, 1981, figs. 49, 50, 53, 55, 57 (ill.)
	Nappi, 1991, p. 161, no. A 84 (ill.)

14. *A City in Ruins at Night,* n.d.
oil on canvas
40¾ x 60¼ in. (103.5 x 154.3 cm)
The Menil Collection, Houston

This painting belongs to a group of representations of ruins for which Nomé has become justly famous. It is hard to ascertain if the group of figures on the left is part of the subject of the painting, or fulfills a merely decorative function. The theatrical light that pervades the canvas and gives it its striking appearance has led some writers to see in this kind of image a variation on the *Vanitas* theme. If this cannot be entirely discounted, one should also be aware of the fortune of such images in the art of Italy and France, from Nomé to Leonardo Coccorante and Viviano Codazzi, and later in the work of Piranesi, Hubert Robert, and Clérisseau, where they are used strictly for decorative purposes.
— J. P. M.

Provenance: Galeria l'Obelisco, Rome, 1950
               Tavazzo collection, Rome
               [Christie's, London]
               Acquired by The Menil Collection in 1963

Exhibitions: Rome, 1950, no. 5
               Houston, 1973–1974, no. 21

Literature: Brion, 1954, p. 6 (ill.)
               J. Bousquet, 1957, p. 2
               Sluys, 1961, no. 107
               Sterling, 1987, pp. 90–91 (ill.)
               Nappi, 1991, p. 118, no. A 57 (ill.)
                   (erroneously located in The Museum of Fine Arts, Houston)

References

Literature

Bier, J. "The Enigma of Monsù Desiderio," *North Carolina Museum of Art Calendar of Events,* vol. 4, no. 11, 1961.

Bousquet, J. "Monsù Desiderio." *Goya,* no. 19, 1957: 2–5.

Bowron, Edgar Peters, ed., *Introduction to the Collections.* Chapel Hill: The University of North Carolina Press, 1983.

Brion, M. "Un peintre peu connu, Monsù Desiderio." *Plaisir de France,* vol. XXI (Febr. 1954): 2, 6.

Brion, M. *L'Art fantastique.* Paris: A. Michel, 1961.

Causa, R. "Francesco Nome detto Monsù Desiderio." *Paragone,* 1956, no. 75: 30–46.

Fredericksen, B. B. and Zeri, F. *Census of Pre-Nineteenth Century Italian Paintings in North American Public Collections.* Cambridge: Harvard University Press, 1972.

Gabhart, A. "Baroque Painting in Italy 1600–1700." *The Bulletin of the Walters Art Gallery,* 1969.

Grate, P. *French Paintings, Seventeenth Century.* Stockholm: Swedish National Art Museums, 1988.

Lebenszejn, J. C. "Une Vanité de Monsù Desiderio." *L'Oeil,* 1967, no. 156: 2–9.

Maltese, C. "Monsù Desiderio Architetto de Rovine," in *Scritti in onore di Leonello Venturi,* vol. 2. Rome, 1956: 65–80.

Nappi, M. R. *François de Nomé e Didier Barra, L'enigma Monsù Desiderio.* Milan, Rome: Jandi Sapi Editori, 1991.

Pariset, F. G. "Monsù Desiderio nel Museo di arti decorativi di Parigi." *Commentarii,* 1952, no. 3: 261–264.

Parthey, G. *Deutscher Bildersaal.* Berlin: Nicolaische Verlaagsbuchhandlung, 1863.

Preiss, P. "Monsù Desiderio, François de Nomé." *Sbornik praci Filosoficke Fakulty Brenske,* XVI, Brno, 1973: 87–95.

The Queens College Art Collection, Queens College, City University of New York. *Images of Destruction: A Selection of Paintings and Prints of Monsù Desiderio and Jacques Callot.* New York: Queens College, 1963.

Réau, L. "Monsù Desiderio." *Bulletin de la Société de l'Histoire de l'Art Français,* 1935, pp. 6–9.

John and Mable Ringling Museum of Art. *The Fantastic Visions of Monsù Desiderio*, foreword by A. Everett Austin, introduction by A. Scharf. Sarasota: The John and Mable Ringling Museum of Art, 1950.

Romdahl A. L. "Notes on Monsù Desiderio." *Göteborgs Hogskolas Arsskrift*, vol. 50, 1944: 1–5.

Rosenberg, Pierre. *France in the Golden Age.* New York: The Metropolitan Museum of Art, 1982.

Roy, C. *Arts Fantastiques.* Paris: R. Delpire, 1960.

Scharf, A. "Once More Monsù." *The Architectural Review*, vol. 105 (Feb. 1949): 91–94.

Scharf, A. "Francesco Desiderio." *The Burlington Magazine*, 1950, no. 92: 18–22.

Seghers, P. *Monsù Desiderio ou le théâtre de la fin du monde.* Paris: R. Laffont, 1981.

Sluys, F. "Monsù Desiderio, peintre de l'irréel." *La vie médicale*, Christmas 1956: 53–63.

Sluys, F. "Un entretien avec le docteur Felix Sluys : Mon diagnostic: l'art fantastique est exutoire des époques intelligentes et inquiètes." *Connaissance des Arts*, 1957, no. 68: 66–73.

Sluys, F. *Didier Barra et François de Nomé dits Monsu Desiderio.* Paris: Editions du Minotaure, n.d. [1961].

Sobotka, G. "Monsù Desiderio," *Thieme-Becker Allgemeines Lexikon der bildenden Künstler.* Leipzig, vol. 9, 1913, p. 131.

Spinosa, N. "Le bizarre et catastrofiche vedute di un Lorenese a Napoli." *Casa Vogue Antiques* (November 1988): 46–49.

Sterling, C. "A City in Ruins at Night." *The Menil Collection: A Selection from the Paleolithic to the Modern Era.* New York, Harry N. Abrams, 1987.

Valentiner, W. R. *Catalogue of Paintings.* Chapel Hill: North Carolina Museum of Art, University of North Carolina Press, 1956.

Van Terey, G. *Die Gemaldegalerie des Museums für bildende Kunste in Budapest.* Berlin: J. Bard, 1916.

Walters, H. *The Walters Collection.* Baltimore: Walters Art Gallery, 1909 (also 1922 and 1929).

Walters Art Gallery. *Treasures of the Walters Art Gallery.* New York: Wildenstein & Co., 1967.

Wright, Christopher. *The French Painters of the 17th Century.* London: Orbis, 1985.

Zeri, F., *Italian Paintings in the Walters Art Gallery.* Baltimore: Walters Art Gallery, 1976, 2 vol.

Zurich Kunsthaus, *Unbekannte Schönheit.* Zurich: Zurich Kunsthaus, 1956.

Exhibitions

Hartford 1940, "Night Scenes," Hartford, The Wadsworth Atheneum.

Rome 1950, "Monsù Desiderio," Rome, Galleria dell'Obelisco.

Sarasota 1950, "The Fantastic Visions of Monsù Desiderio," Sarasota, John and Mable Ringling Museum of Art.

Saarbrück and Rouen 1954, "Chefs-d'œuvre oubliés ou peu connus," Saarbrück, Saarland Museum; Rouen, Musée des Beaux-Arts.

Zurich, 1956, "Unbekannte Schönheit," Zurich Kunsthaus.

Bordeaux 1957, "Exposition du fantastique de Bosch à Goya," Bordeaux, Musée de Beaux-Arts.

Dallas 1961, "The Art That Broke the Looking Glass," The Dallas Museum for Contemporary Arts.

Houston 1961, "Desiderio's Cathedral," Houston, University of St. Thomas, Fine Arts Department.

New York 1962, "Scenes and spectacles: The Theater World of the Baroque," New York, Queens College, Paul Klapper Library.

New York 1963–64, "Images of Destruction: A Selection of Paintings and Prints of Monsu Desiderio and Jacques Callot," New York, The Queens College Art Collection, Queens College, The City University of New York.

Houston 1964, "Out of This World: An Exhibition of Fantastic Landscapes from the Renaissance to the Present," Houston, University of St. Thomas, Fine Arts Gallery.

New York 1967, "Treasures of the Walters Art Gallery," Wildenstein, New York.

Houston 1971–72, "Selections from the Menil Collection," Houston, Rice University, Institute for the Arts.

Houston 1973–1974, "Gray is the Color: An exhibition of grisaille paintings XIII–XXth centuries," Houston, Rice University, Institute for the Arts.

Houston 1979–80, "Day and Night: Works from the Menil Foundation Collection," Houston, Institute for the Arts, Rice University, Houston.

Nice 1982, "Le temple, représentation de l'architecture sacrée," Nice, Musée Cheret.

Paris–New York–Chicago 1982, "La peinture française du XVIIe siècle dans les collections américaines," Paris, Galeries Nationales du Grand-Palais; New York, The Metropolitan Museum of Art; Chicago, The Art Institute of Chicago, 1982.

Paris 1984, "La rime et la raison: les collections Ménil," Paris, Galeries Nationales du Grand Palais.

Naples 1984–85, "Civiltà del Seicento a Napoli," Naples, Soprintendenza dei beni Culturali.

Stockholm 1988, "Poussin oc haus... 1600 ital.," Stockholm, Nationalmuseum.

Photo Credits

Fig. 1, courtesy of the Sibergnagl Collections; fig. 2, courtesy of Jandi Sapi Editori, Milan, Rome; fig. 3, courtesy of Archive Photographie, Paris/SPADEM; fig. 4, Cathy Carver; fig. 5, courtesy of Art Resource, New York; pl. 1, courtesy of North Carolina Museum of Art, Raleigh; pl. 2, Christine Guest, Montreal; pls. 3, 4, L. Sully-Jaulmes; pl. 5, T. R. Du Brock; pls. 6, 7, courtesy of Walters Art Gallery, Baltimore; pl. 8, courtesy of Nationalmuseum, Stockholm; pl. 9, Josepf Szaszfai, New Haven; pl. 10, A. Rázsó, Budapest; pls. 11, 14, Hickey-Robertson, Houston; pl. 12, courtesy of owner; pl. 13, courtesy of the Fitzwilliam Museum, Cambridge.

Design
Don Quaintance, Public Address Design, Houston
Elizabeth Frizzell, Production Assistant

Composition and Typography
John Kaiser, Editorial Associate, The Menil Collection
with Arvin C. Conrad, computer consultant to the Menil Foundation
Composed in Autologic Galliard at T$_{\!E}$Xsource, Houston

Printing
W.E. Barnett and Associates, Houston

Color separations and halftones
Color Separations, Inc. Houston

Binding
Roswell Bookbinders, Phoenix